Seeing Things

By the end of this book you will know more about:

- How we can see.
- How light changes direction.
- Shadows and reflections.

You will:

- Use Fact Files, books and CD-ROMs to help you answer questions.
- Carry out tests.
- Record results in tables and draw line graphs.

Light travels from a source.

Fact File

Total darkness

Task 1

Daisy sees a monster

1

Daisy went down to the dark cellar. She shone her torch around. Her father's boiler suit was hanging on a hook. Its shadow gave her a terrible shock.

 Use Task Sheet 1 to explain how this shadow was made.

Use all these words:

light source	opaque
light travelling	block

 Draw a diagram. Show how the shadow was made.

Have you ever been in total darkness? Not the darkness of your bedroom, or the street at night. They seem dark, but there is still enough light to see. Total darkness is the darkness of a dungeon, a coal mine or a cave. You can see nothing – not even your hand in front of your face!

In total darkness you need a light source to see. You need a torch or a candle. Even a match will give you some light. When the light goes out, you are in total darkness again. Without the light, you can see nothing.

Fact File

Eyes

When you go into a darkened room on a sunny day, you can see nothing at first. Your eyes are used to the bright light outside. The **pupils** – the holes in the centre of your eyes that appear black – are tiny, protecting your eyes from the brightness by allowing very little light in. This is because the **iris** – the coloured part of your eyes – is nearly closed. But in the darkness, your iris expands and your pupils get bigger, to let in the light that filters through the curtains or shines under the door. Now you can see again. You may think that you can 'see in the dark', but you are really seeing with the tiny amount of light in the darkened room.

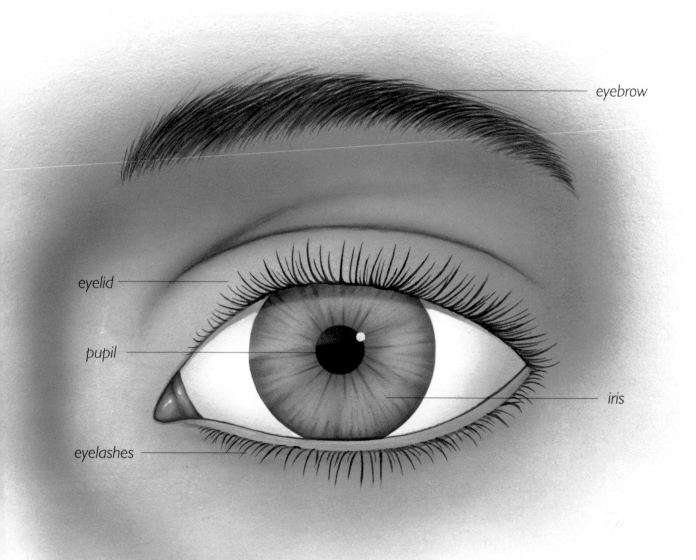

The human eye

We see because light from a source enters our eyes.

Angharad's grandfather

Angharad's grandfather used to be a coal miner. One day, he took a strange white hat from his cupboard.

"This is my coal mining helmet," he told Angharad. "There is a lamp on the helmet, and a battery in this box. Would you like to try it?"

Angharad put the helmet on. It was heavy, and Angharad's head was weighed down. Her grandfather began to laugh.

"What's so funny?" asked Angharad.

"You've put it on back to front!" said her grandfather. "It would be no use to you like that. Your eyes are at the front, but the lamp is at the back!"

Angharad was puzzled. "What's the problem?" she wondered.

Tell Angharad why the lamp is on the front of the helmet. Explain why it is useful to have a lamp on your hat, not in your hand. Describe what will happen as she turns her head to look at things.

You need a light source to see

Stephanie, Michael and Yasmin were arguing about how you see things. They each had a different idea. They drew their ideas.

Stephanie's idea:
You see things when the light from your eye reaches them.

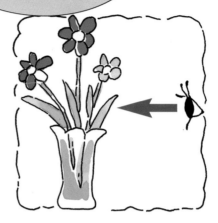

Michael's idea:
The light in the room is reflected from your eye so that you can see things.

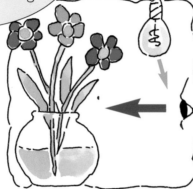

Yasmin's idea:
The light is reflected by the flowers (and from everything else). Some of the light enters your eyes.

✪ What do you think happens?

✪ Complete Task Sheet 2.

The safety lamp

Before electric light was available, miners took candles down the mine with them. They strapped lighted candles to the front of their hats. But they were in danger from a gas called 'firedamp'. The firedamp caught fire easily or exploded. The scientist Sir Humphry Davy invented a safety lamp that burned in the mine without setting the firedamp alight. What can you find out in CD-ROMs, books and on the Internet about Sir Humphry Davy and his famous 'Davy Lamp'?

A Davy lamp

Mirrors reflect light into our eyes.
Draw straight lines with arrows to show the direction of
travelling light.

Task 4 ## Through the looking glass

In Lewis Carroll's *Alice Through the Looking Glass*, Alice arrives in a mysterious country on the other side of the mirror, where everything is reversed. As you know, mirrors reflect light and images. When you see objects in a mirror, the light travels from the object to the mirror and then to your eyes. With a mirror, you can see behind you and you can see round things. We can recognise things and people in mirrors, but their images are reversed.

✦ What is reversed in this picture?

To show how light travels from a light source you can draw a straight line with an arrow, The arrow tip shows the direction of the light.

✦ Why is the arrow always straight?

Tricks with a mirror

Here are some things you can do with a safety mirror.

✦ Try them out. Think about the light's journey from its source to your eyes. Decide where the light is reflected.

- Look at your own teeth.

- Use a mirror like a cap peak. Watch your feet as you walk along but make sure you don't bump into things!

- Turn your back on the classroom board. See what's on the board.

- Look under your table without bending over.

- Look round a corner.

- Look at your own eyes.

✦ Draw a sketch of what you did. Use arrows to show the light's journey. Remember to draw straight lines.

> **Words to learn and use:**
> iris
> light source
> opaque
> pupil
> reflect

Fact File

There are many uses for mirrors. You may use one in the bathroom to help you wash and clean your teeth – after all, you won't see your own teeth without one! Drivers use mirrors on cars to reflect what is behind them, or by the roadside to see round corners. Shopkeepers use mirrors to see all around the shop.

Mirrors around you

⭐ **Light beams change direction when reflected from surfaces. Make careful observations and comparisons.**

Snooker balls and light beams

When a snooker ball hits the cushion at the side of the table, it is deflected and bounces away. A good snooker player can bounce the ball at the exact angle they want, so that the snooker ball goes into the pocket. Snooker players can do this because they know that snooker balls travel in a straight line – in fact, the snooker ball behaves like a light beam.

Light is reflected like the snooker ball. Light hits a mirror in a straight line, and 'bounces' from the mirror in a straight line. You can change the direction of the 'bounce' by changing the angle of the mirror. You can use this to play a game.

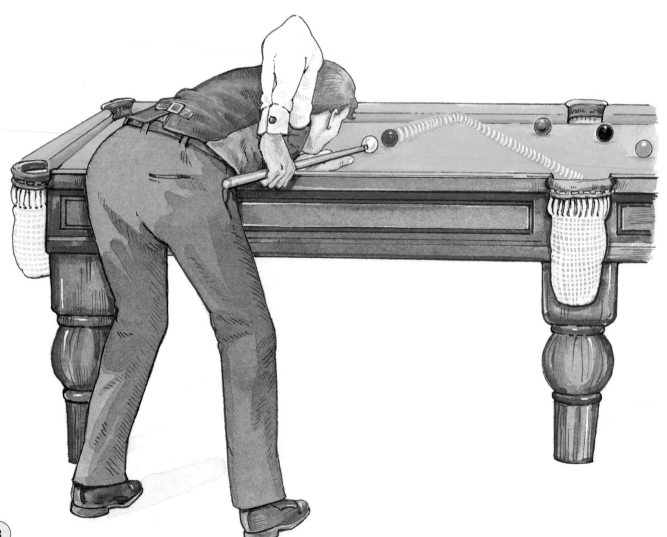

Scientific Enquiry
Light snooker

This activity works best in a darkened or shady part of the classroom.

What to do:

1 Lay the white paper on the table, and place the torch on top of it. Tape the card to the torch so that a thin light beam shines through the slot across the table.

2 Put the target on the table.

3 Switch off the torch.

4 Place the mirror so that a beam reflected from it will hit the target.

5 Switch on the torch. Were you right?

You can make the game harder by switching the torch off before placing both the mirror and the target.

What did you find? Make drawings to show what you found out. You could use a computer package to create your drawings or create a web page to show other children how light is reflected.

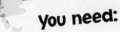

you need:

• bright torch

• piece of card with a slot cut in it

• tape

• large sheet of white paper

• plastic mirror standing up in a piece of Blu-tack

• target (something to aim your light beam at)

Shiny surfaces reflect light better than dull surfaces. Compare how different surfaces reflect light.

 Task 7

 3

Everything reflects light but you notice reflections best on shiny surfaces. Smooth polished surfaces can act like mirrors – they reflect an image. Dull or rough surfaces do not produce a clear image.

✦ Look carefully at the objects you have collected. Are they shiny or dull?

✦ Complete Task Sheet 3.

Extra Challenge

✦ Look at the photographs.

✦ Use the aluminium foil to present a trick called 'The Disappearing Image'.

you need:

- torch
- plastic mirror
- smooth aluminium foil
- crumpled aluminium foil
- shiny plastic
- sheet of paper
- piece of wood
- piece of cloth

Shiny surfaces are attractive

Most people like a well-polished surface. People like shiny furniture and shiny cars. Cooks glaze food with egg, sugar or butter to give it a shine and make it attractive. The smooth reflective surface of still water makes the water look perfect for a swim.

At Christmas, everything has a shine: tree decorations sparkle, wrapping paper and holly leaves shine, and even the snow glistens.

Try to think of other shiny things that you find attractive.

Christmas decorations sparkle

Shiny food looks good

CDs are smooth and shiny

A polished car gleams

You can change the size and position of an object's shadow. Consider trends in results and decide whether some results don't fit the pattern.

Check measurements by repeating them.

 Task **8**

Investigating shadows

 4

Class 6 were planning a shadow puppet show.

"It would be very scary if we made the villain grow really big!" said Ed.
"How can we do that?" asked Will.
"If we move the puppet behind the screen, it's shadow will get bigger." said Ed.
"Move it which way?" asked Will.
"What do you mean? asked Ed.
"Towards the screen or away from it?"
"Oh I don't know. We'd better try it."

Now it's your turn to investigate this problem.

To investigate Will and Ed's problem you will need to decide:

- what you are changing.

- a measurement you are recording after each change.

- what you should keep the same.

Copy and complete the table. Write **changing, measuring** or **same** in each box.

 you need:

- cardboard figure

- bright torch or OHP

- screen or wall

- ruler to measure distances and size of the shadow

Words to learn and use:
dull
glaze
light beam
mirror
polished
shadows
shiny

Height of puppet	Distance of figure from light	Angle of puppet	Brightness of light	Angle of screen	Height of shadow

☆ Carry out the investigation.

☆ Complete Task Sheet 4 and draw a line graph from your results.

- Put the measurement you are changing along the horizontal x-axis.

- Put the measurement you are recording after each change along the vertical y-axis.

- Plot the points for your measurements.

☆ Can you join the points with one line? Is there a pattern?

☆ Are you surprised by where some of the points are? Should you try measuring these points again?

☆ Write down what you found out from your graph.

Will and Ed had their own ideas:

"The nearer the light, the bigger the shadow," said Ed.

"The nearer the screen, the smaller the shadow," said Will.

"The stronger the light, the bigger the shadow."

"The further from the light, the smaller the shadow."

☆ Were they right?

Shadows and reflections are different.

 Task 9 Black reflections

....

 5

Nicola's little brother had his own ideas about shadows.

"Shadows are like black reflections," he said.

"It's not quite like that," said Nicola. "Shadows and reflections are two different things. Let me explain…"

✴ Complete Task Sheet 5 to help Nicola explain.

"Here are some pictures," said Nicola. "They will help you understand."

✴ Draw some pictures to help Nicola's little brother understand reflections.

Checkpoint

Up periscope!

A periscope is used to see over things.

On Task Sheet 6 draw three straight arrows that show how the periscope reflects light.

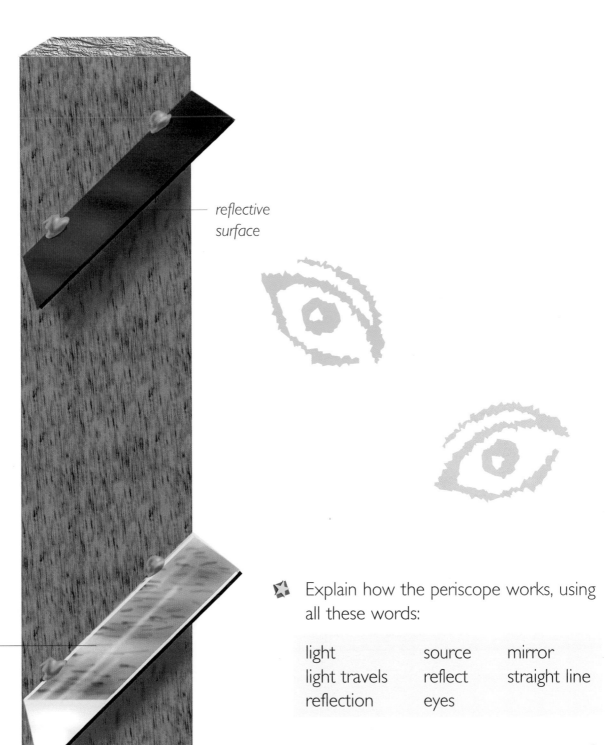

reflective surface

reflective surface

Explain how the periscope works, using all these words:

light	source	mirror
light travels	reflect	straight line
reflection	eyes	

Summary

Which of these do you know and which can you do?

- I know that light travels from a source.
- I know that we see because light from a source enters our eyes.
- I know that mirrors reflect light into our eyes.
- I can draw straight lines with arrows to show the direction of travelling light.
- I know that light beams change direction when they are reflected from surfaces.
- I can make careful observations and comparisons.
- I know that shiny surfaces reflect light better than dull surfaces.
- I can compare how different surfaces reflect light.
- I know how to change the size and position of an object's shadow.
- I can consider trends in results and decide whether some results don't fit the pattern.
- I can check measurements by repeating them.
- I know that shadows and reflections are different.

Complete your **Science Log** to show how well you know these and how well you can do them. Circle a face for each statement.